SIMPLY BEAUTIFUL

JERRY RAY

Simply Beautiful has brought me more pleasure and musical enjoyment than almost any other project in which I've been involved. To become so close and intimate with the most beautiful melodies ever written, by some of the most gifted composers, has allowed me hours of musical exhilaration. The approach was to stay true to the composer's original intent, yet "extend" the piece into a more contemporary arrangement.

My favorite? Well, as a young piano student my teacher assigned the composition "To a Wild Rose." At first I didn't care for the piece, until I realized how incredibly beautiful a simple little melody could be. As I look back, I can say that "To a Wild Rose" was the work that made the little light go on in my head, and I finally realized that music was more than black printer's ink on a page— it was heart, it was soul and it was passion. What a concept!

Begin *Simply Beautiful* by starting with one piece at a time, then slowly make friends with them all. Savor the simplistic freshness and total uniqueness inherent to each. Become mesmerized by the musical magic to be discovered in every note. Allow yourself to be captivated by the warmth and comfort in each passage. Perhaps one of these selections will make that little musical light in your head get just a little brighter, like it did in mine. That would be *Simply Beautiful*.

Enjoy!

Jerry Ray

Contents

Copyright © MCMXCII by Alfred Publishing Co., Inc.

Cover Art: James Buckels
With special thanks to Robley Wilson, editor,
The North American Review

REVERIE

Andante–with much expression

Claude Debussy
Arr. by Jerry Ray

4

BLUE DANUBE

Johann Strauss
Arr. by Jerry Ray

POLOVETSIAN DANCE

Alexander Borodin
Arr. by Jerry Ray

TALES FROM THE VIENNA WOODS

Johann Strauss
Arr. by Jerry Ray

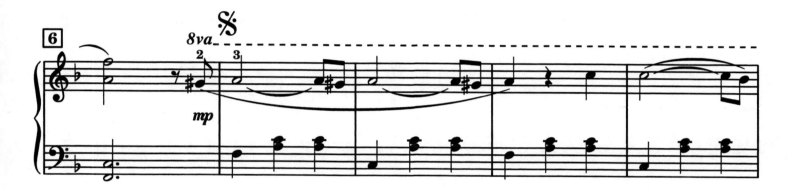

(Continue 8va until measure 51.)

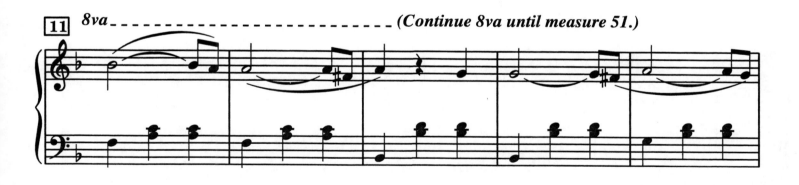

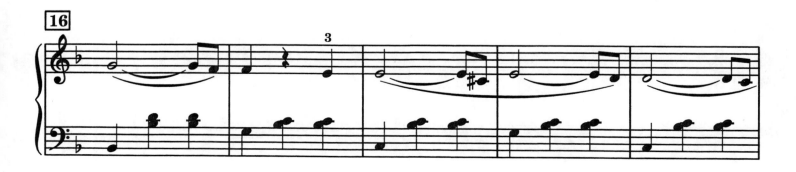

THE SWAN

Camille Saint-Saëns
Arr. by Jerry Ray

Slowly–with much expression

THEME FROM
ROMEO AND JULIET

Peter Ilyich Tchaikovsky
Arr. by Jerry Ray

Andante espressivo

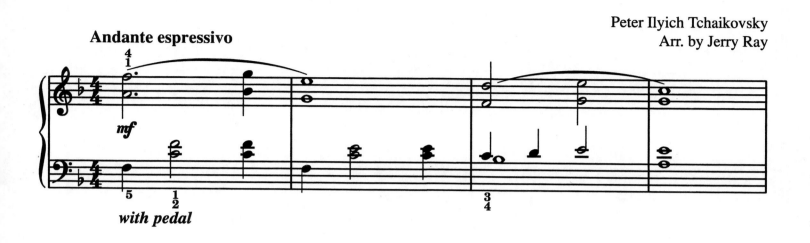

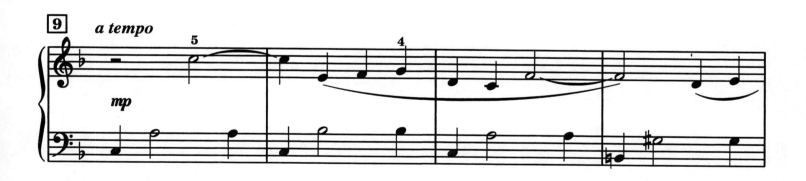

18

CLAIR DE LUNE

Claude Debussy
Arr. by Jerry Ray

With much expression*

*To accommodate the style and approach of this book, the time signature has been changed from 9/8.

MUSETTA'S WALTZ

(from La Bohème)

Giacomo Puccini
Arr. by Jerry Ray

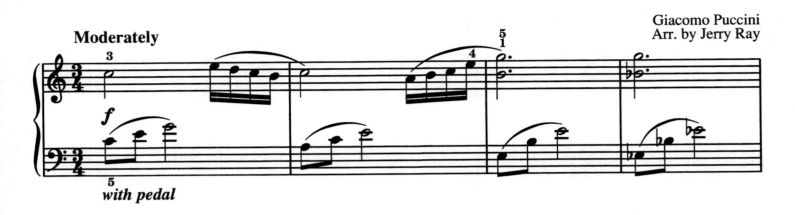

AIR FOR THE G STRING

Johann Sebastian Bach
Arr. by Jerry Ray

TO A WILD ROSE

Edward MacDowell
Arr. by Jerry Ray

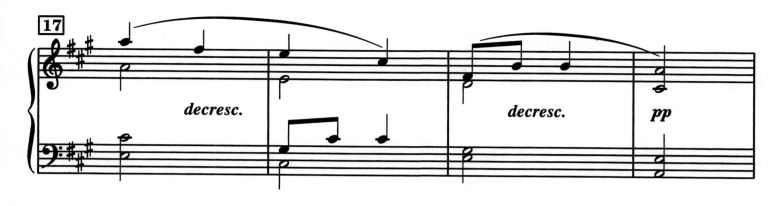

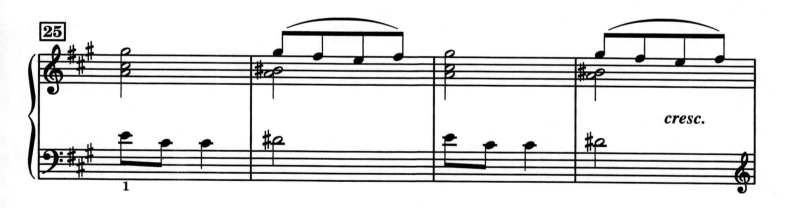